Children of the Incas

Children of

by David Mangurian

the Incas

FOUR WINDS PRESS   NEW YORK

985
Man

I am grateful to UNICEF for the assignment that started this project; to Judy Whipple, who had faith enough in my work to give me a contract for the book; to Portogallo Photographic Services of New York City for beautiful prints; to my editor, Beverly Reingold, for finally getting the book out of me; and to my wife, Luz, who faithfully transcribed Modesto's words, helped on the fine points of translation and cultural interpretation, and encouraged me throughout my work.

LIBRARY OF CONGRESS CATALOGING IN PUBLICATION DATA

Mangurian, David.
   Children of the Incas.
   SUMMARY: A 13-year-old Quechua Indian boy living in a village near Lake Titicaca describes his family, home, and day-to-day activities.
   1. Quechua Indians — Juvenile literature. 2. Quispe Mamani, Modesto — Juvenile literature. 3. Quechua Indians — Biography — Juvenile literature. [1. Quechua Indians. 2. Indians of South America. 3. Peru — Social life and customs] I. Title.
F2230.2.K4M37   980'.004'98   79-12186
ISBN 0-590-07500-4

Published by Four Winds Press
A division of Scholastic Magazines, Inc., New York, N.Y.
Copyright © 1979 by David Mangurian
All rights reserved
Printed in the United States of America
Library of Congress Catalog Card Number: 79-12186
2   3   4   5   83   82   81

To the people of Coata

Children of the Incas

THE TOWN OF COATA (pronounced Co-AH-ta) is not even a dot on the map of Peru. According to a 1975 census, there were 104 people, 192 sheep, 92 pigs, 80 cows, and 28 chickens living within the town limits. But Coata is the civic and commercial center for about 7,000 people living in the surrounding countryside.

Coata is located near Lake Titicaca, 3,820 meters above sea level on the great plateau in the middle of South America called the *altiplano*. It is one of the poorest regions of the world. A whooping cough epidemic killed 600 children and adults in the Coata district in 1970. One out of every three children dies before his first birthday.

I went to Coata for the first time to photograph Indian life for UNICEF. For years I had photographed Indians in Latin America. But I had never really gotten to know any. The only way you get to know people is by sleeping in their homes, eating their food, and living their routine.

I decided to live with an Indian family in Coata. I found a farmer named Juan Dionicio Quispe who had an empty adobe hut. He agreed to put me up. I agreed to pay for my food and lodging.

Juan and his wife, Narcisa, had five children, ranging in age from thirteen to three. I liked the kids right off. They were excited about my staying with them. I think I was the big event in Coata that week.

The family lived together with Narcisa's parents, her brother and his family, and her unmarried youngest sister in a compound of eight small adobe huts built around a dirt patio. The front of the compound faced a street and the back faced the flat tundra of the *altiplano*.

The families shared many things, but each had its own living quarters. Two of the huts were kitchens. One of the huts on the street side of the compound was Juan's store. It did so little business it was opened only when a customer came knocking.

My hut measured about three meters by five meters. It, like the other huts, had a dirt floor, a thatched roof, no windows, and a wooden frame door with galvanized sheet metal nailed to it. My bed was a platform made of dried, brick-hard adobe. On a ledge in one corner was a pile of dried cow dung the family burned as firewood for cooking. It did not smell. The family's bathroom, which I shared, was the ground in back of the compound of huts next to the wall of the sheep pen.

Modesto, the eldest child in the family, brought dinner to my hut that first evening. It was a bowl of potato and barley soup with *chuños*. *Chuños* are made during winter by putting potatoes out on the tundra to freeze overnight, stepping on them the next day to squeeze out the water, and then letting them dry in the sun.

I had three candles lighting my room. Modesto stayed to watch me eat. He was terribly curious. We talked, getting to know each other. After I finished, he took my bowl away and returned with a cup of hot tea made from coca leaves. Coca leaves contain the drug cocaine. But as a tea, coca leaves produce nothing more than a mild medicinal effect good for stomach pains. My cup of coca-leaf tea had lots of sugar in it. It tasted good.

When I finally finished, Modesto said: "Do you want me to stay with you tonight?"

I was a little shocked at the suggestion. "No," I told him. Shortly, he said good night and left me alone.

It was cold. The wind was blowing outside my door. I was glad there were no windows in the hut. I got into my sleeping bag. My mattress was three heavy woolen ponchos and a reed mat. I had two ponchos over me. I had on underwear, thermal underwear over that, pajamas, thermal socks, and a woolen sweater. I was still cold.

Then I understood why Modesto had offered to sleep with me. The more bodies in the same bed, the warmer you sleep.

I stayed with the Quispe family four nights and four days. Modesto and his younger brother, Romoldo, spoke pretty good Spanish and were my constant companions.

Juan spoke Spanish poorly, but we could talk. He was proud to show me how they lived. Whenever he began to do something I hadn't seen before, he would get me so I could photograph it.

Narcisa and the three daughters spoke only Quechua, the same language the Incas used. But kids are kids in any language. The two little sisters, Celestina and Melania, hung around me and giggled every time I looked at them. They loved to play with my empty, bright-yellow Kodak film boxes.

All the kids loved to play ball on the tundra in back of the family compound. They liked me to kick it around with

them, but the air was so rare at that altitude that I would tire out quickly. They didn't.

Most of the time, however, everyone except the two little girls were working at something. The family had five sources of income:

1. Sharecropping on several tiny plots of land as far as two hours' walking distance from the compound.
2. Tending sheep.

3. Selling boiled fish, potatoes, and *chuños* in the plaza on market days.
4. Running the small store.
5. Knitting woolen sweaters sold through the government's handicraft center.

The government had recently started a handicraft program in Coata to help the Indians supplement their farming income, so dependent on the unpredictable weather. The Quispe family went into it whole hog. Narcisa and Santusa, the eldest daughter, spun yarn from wool. Juan, Modesto, and Romoldo knit the sweaters.

The family spun yarn and knit while walking out to the fields and back, while tending the sheep, while resting from other work. Modesto and Romoldo knit even while kicking around their soccer ball.

I tried to determine how much money the family earned a year, but it was difficult. Juan did not keep account books. He could barely write. But based on what Juan and Modesto told me and what I saw, my guess is that the family earned the equivalent of about $500 a year, not counting the food they raised for their own consumption.

After the first night, I asked to eat my meals with the family in their hut. Narcisa and Santusa never ate with us. They stayed in the smoky kitchen hut, keeping the food hot.

We had breakfast shortly after the sun came up. As soon as

the sun rises above the *altiplano* horizon, it is bright daylight because the atmosphere is so thin.

Breakfast was always the same — a couple of triangular rolls, very weak coffee with lots of sugar, and toasted whole wheat kernels that we ate with our hands like popcorn. It was the best meal of the day.

About two hours later we'd eat "lunch." The first time I ate lightly, expecting another meal at noon. There was no other lunch. They ate early out of habit, Modesto said, because when they went out to the fields they couldn't cook a midday meal.

Lunch, like dinner, was often potato and barley soup with *chuños*. I soon told Narcisa to "hold the *chuños*." I couldn't stand their taste or texture.

A couple of times we had quinoa, a tiny yellowish bean which tasted like salty Cream of Wheat cereal. Once I found a couple of small pieces of hard-boiled egg in my bowl of quinoa. Narcisa had cut up one egg for the eight of us. It was the only egg I ever saw. We never had milk or chicken or beef or pork or lamb or green vegetables or any fruit.

During my stay in Coata, people didn't ask me many questions. A lot of them did not know where the United States was. But they did know the United States had put men on the moon, and they asked about that.

At times, Coata seemed as removed from my way of life as

the moon was from theirs. No telephones ever rang. No buses ever came through town. The postmaster told me he received eight to ten letters a week — for the entire district! And nearly everybody could relate some experience with a sorcerer.

In the evenings I would invite Modesto into my hut and ask him questions about his life, recording everything on a tape recorder. I wanted this story to be in Modesto's words, because a person's life is more real when he tells about it himself. Modesto knew what I was doing and wanted the book to be good. Several times he told me, "I want people where you live to *know* how we live."

So here, as faithfully as I could edit and translate them, are Modesto's own words.

My name is Modesto Quispe Mamani. I'm thirteen years old. I am one meter, forty centimeters tall. I have a soccer ball and a watch my father bought me in the market for school. Sure, I complain sometimes. But I'm not a bad guy.

I was born here in the highlands. Everyone lives so far apart here. It's very quiet. There's no shouting. Hardly anything exciting ever happens. It's as if people were standing around in a daze.

Highland people are kind of stubborn. You could say they're a little stupid. Some people around here still believe that the earth is flat! They think that the sun goes around the earth.

It's said that years ago our ancestors lived just like wild animals. They didn't know how to plant the fields. They didn't know how to build houses. They didn't even know how to cook.

Then Manco Capac and Mama Ocllo rose out of the waters of Lake Titicaca. Manco Capac was the first Inca. And Mama Ocllo was his wife.

Manco Capac taught the men how to plant the fields. He taught them how to build houses and how to make things. He taught them how to work.

And Mama Ocllo taught the women how to cook. She taught them how to make and wash clothes. She taught them how to raise children.

Manco Capac and Mama Ocllo taught the people all those things. It's true. They taught our ancestors how to live.

My father is Juan Dionicio. He's a farmer. Sometimes he's a little grouchy, but he's a kind person. He loves us. He never whips us like some fathers do. I think it's because his father didn't whip him.

My mother's name is Narcisa. She's always cheerful, except when somebody in her family dies. She hardly ever spanks us. But sometimes she makes us go without dinner for not hauling water from the river. When she was a little girl, she used to go hungry a lot.

My grandfather is nice. He never went to school, but he can read your fortune from coca leaves. He's a farmer, too, just like his father and his grandfather and his grandfather's father. They all planted potatoes and barley and wheat and grazed sheep the same as we do.

My family, my Uncle Luis and his family, and my Aunt Modesta live with my grandfather and my grandmother. We all have separate houses, but my grandfather owns the property.

We don't have much of a house. The bedroom is also the dining room. My three sisters sleep there with my father and my mother. My brother Romoldo and I used to sleep there, too. But now we sleep in our store.

One time my father and my mother brought home boxes of new pants and sweaters and hats to sell in the store. The next day was the Feast of Jesus of Nazareth, when everybody in the district comes into town. The store was filled with stuff. They had worked five years to buy all the things.

That night, while everybody was sleeping, thieves broke into the store and stole everything. The clothes, money, bottles of beer and liquor, coca leaves, soft drinks. They even took my parents' documents and photographs.

My mother and father searched everywhere. They found some empty suitcases down behind the cemetery and some more over near the river. They found boxes scattered all over the place. But they didn't find any of the clothes or other things. Nothing.

My father reported the robbery to the judge, but the authorities didn't catch the thieves. My parents finally went to a sorcerer. He told them the ringleader of the thieves was a man named Julian Pacampía, who lived outside of town. The sorcerer said he would cast a spell and the man would die. He told my parents to go to the church tower.

My parents went to the church tower that afternoon. And there was the man, Julian Pacampía! Soon afterward, he died. Ever since that day, there haven't been many robberies in Coata.

My parents have never replaced what they lost. There's not enough money. We don't have much in the store anymore. But Romoldo and I sleep there so it won't be robbed again.

21

Romoldo is in the fourth grade. He doesn't study very hard. He's not interested. He'd rather knit sweaters than study.

Whenever we play together, he wants to win. Cards, ball, whatever. He doesn't like me to beat him. He gets mad.

My sister Santusa is in the first grade. She can't speak Spanish yet, only Quechua. She's afraid to speak Spanish. Santusa doesn't like school. Sometimes girls here don't even finish grade school.

But does she know how to have fun! She plays all the time. I love to play with her.

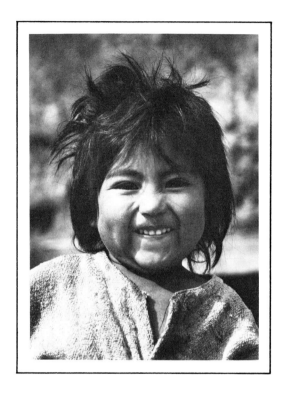 

Celestina is almost three years old.

Melania is going to be four.

They're like twins. If we buy a doll for one and not the other, they fight over the doll. Last Christmas Celestina got a ball and a doll. Melania got the same.

My little sisters, they just play all day long.

I used to have two other sisters. Their names were Simeona and Rafaela. They were about the same size as Melania and Celestina are now. Simeona was five. The other was three.

They got sick one September. They got headaches, then fever, stomach pains, a cough. We didn't know what they had. They came down with it fast.

I don't remember everything. I was still young. I got sick, too, but my godmother cured me.

My sisters were sick about a week. The youngest one, Rafaela, died first. She died on a Thursday at four in the morning. We buried her on Friday.

Lots of people were dying. Six, eight, ten. Up to a dozen every day. Every day there were burials. Children, and grown-ups, too.

On Sunday, Simeona was still very sick. She

had a terrible cough. There was a mass for the soul of my father's father. My mother went to where my father's family lived to go to church with them.

Simeona got worse. So my father decided to take her to the church to hear the mass. As he was passing the entrance to the handicraft center, he stopped. He says her eyes rolled back and she stopped breathing. She died there in his arms. It was about ten o'clock in the morning.

Weeping, my father brought her back to the house and left her. I was still in bed getting better. Then my mother and my grandparents and Simeona's godparents came. They were weeping. They wrapped her in a shroud and stayed all night burning candles for her. The next day they buried her.

My father said nothing. He went to hear mass. And he cried all week. What bad luck that they died.

People come from all over the district to bury the dead in our cemetery. They take the body to the church, and then they carry it to the cemetery and place it inside a little house we call purgatory. The soul of the body rests there while they dig the grave.

The first person ever to die in Coata was buried inside that little house. Nobody remembers anymore who it was. Not even my grandfather.

Then the daughter of a man named Avila died. He lived near the lake, two hours' walking distance from here. He had plenty of cattle. He was very wealthy. So he paid the mayor and the town council to dig up the bones of the first dead person, so that he could bury his daughter inside the little house in the cemetery.

Whenever they dig a new grave now, they find bones. They used to put them inside the little house. Now they don't bother. They just bury the old bones again with the new bodies. The cemetery is full.

Once there was nothing here. Just a family named Coasaca. One day the Virgin Mary appeared to them in a vision. Since there was not even a chapel, they built a little one for the Virgin. Then

Fray Velasco came and founded the town and named it Coata after the family, Coasaca. That was in 1854.

Now Coata has . . .

A church

A school up to the fifth grade

A handicraft center

A post office

A district governor and his lieutenants

A mayor and town council

A justice of the peace to settle disagreements

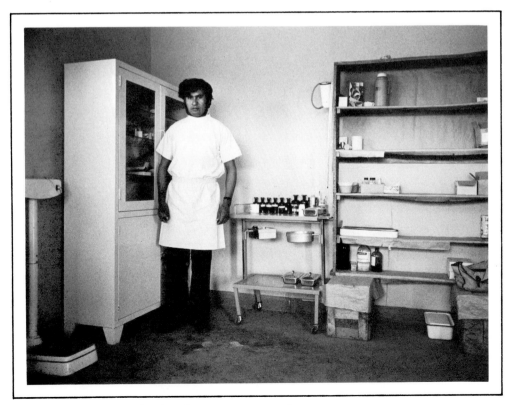

A health post where the nurse works

And streets, and a plaza! Peddlers from the city come to the plaza every Wednesday with clothes and vegetables and fruit. My mother sells boiled fish and potatoes at the market. People from all over the district come in to Coata. Sometimes they buy their children a banana or an orange.

I'm in the fifth grade. School begins at nine. We have to be on time, or the teacher makes us run through the "Dark Alley." That's where all the boys line up and take off their belts and whip the one who was late.

I've been late twice. They went easy on me because they're all my friends. But some kids have quarrels with others. They get hit hard. Even the girls.

On the weekends Romoldo and I take care of the sheep. Once we got caught in a hailstorm. It was clear and sunny when we took the sheep out, so we didn't bother to take our ponchos or our hats.

At noon it got cloudy and started thundering. But we were fooling around playing ball. Suddenly it began to hail. The hailstones were pounding us and the sheep didn't want to move. We were freezing cold.

All of a sudden, a hailstone the size of a rock hit me on the head. I felt as if my head had split open. Then we saw my father running toward us. In a couple of minutes he arrived with our jackets and our ponchos and a piece of plastic to cover us from the rain and the hail.

When we got home, my head hurt worse. I touched it. There was a huge bump. It hurt for three days. It still hurts when I remember that day.

It hails a lot here. That's why we don't put any windows in our houses. The hail would break the glass and the frost would come in at night. It gets very cold. You feel it right to your bones.

Another time we lost a sheep. It was a Saturday. Romoldo and I took the sheep out to graze. They were eating peacefully, so we played ball the whole day. We always fool around. Without our noticing, one of the sheep crossed over to another flock. It was a big sheep, too.

Late in the afternoon we brought our flock in. When we got home, my father said: "There's one sheep missing. Where's the sheep?"

It startled us because we didn't know we had lost a sheep.

Then he said: "Go back out and look for it."

We went back, but we couldn't find it. It got dark and we had to come in.

Well, my father wasn't angry. He doesn't get angry at us. But he said: "If you don't find the sheep, you're going to get your first whipping."

That night I didn't sleep well. I was scared.

The next morning, after breakfast, Romoldo and I went out to look for the sheep again. All day long we walked around asking people: "Have you seen it? Has it been sold?"

Everyone answered, "No."

Some people who had been grazing their sheep
the day before had not brought them back to graze.
So at about three o'clock in the afternoon, we went
to their house. And there, grazing with their sheep
in another pasture, we found our sheep. The people
said they had not noticed it.

We ran all the way back home with the sheep,
laughing and playing and jumping in the fields. We
were so happy. My father didn't whip us. He was
happy, too.

On New Year's Day we usually slaughter a sheep. We do it on birthdays, too, sometimes.

My father and my grandfather tie up the legs so the sheep won't kick. Then one of them cuts its throat with a knife. They catch the blood in a washbasin. Sometimes we cook it. Sometimes we give it to the dog.

Then they cut off the feet and blow in the legs to puff up the body. They wait a moment and then cut the belly open. They pull off the skin and take out the intestines. We eat those, too.

We don't eat meat very often because we don't own many animals. Most of our sheep belong to a woman from the city. She and her brothers own all the pastureland around here. We're her caretakers. My grandfather has served her for years.

She comes and has us slaughter one or two sheep and takes the meat away to market. She leaves us the intestines. Same with the cows. In return for taking care of her animals, the woman lets us graze our own animals on her land. We don't have any other place for them to feed.

We also farm on her land. The woman brings the seed. We do the work. Half the harvest is ours. The other half belongs to her.

When we plant the crops, we all go to the fields. We plant the potatoes in November and December. My father digs holes with a spade and my mother follows, putting in the potatoes. Then

they cover them over with soil. When they hurry, sometimes the spade cuts my mother's fingers and she bleeds.

My parents and my grandparents and my uncles and aunts all chew coca leaves when they work in the fields. They say it gives them more strength. When the cold winds make their heads ache, they say coca makes the pain go away. They say coca keeps them from feeling hungry.

My mother buys it by the bushel and they all divide it up. It's expensive. Each person chews half a pound a day.

My grandfather says he learned to chew coca when he was a kid because there wasn't much food then.

One time I said to myself: "I wonder what coca is like." So I took some from my father's bag and hid by myself. I tried just a little bit. After a minute I had to spit it out. It was like eating paper.

How could I ever be a gentleman someday if I chewed coca leaves all the time?

When I was in the third grade, I went to live with my uncle in Arequipa. It's a beautiful city. People live in nice rooms and they have electricity. They earn a monthly salary. Kids can buy whatever they want. There's a soccer stadium.

City people see everything. They run around the streets talking and shouting, saying whatever they think. They know all the news.

I stayed in Arequipa two years. In the highlands the sun and the cold turn our skin dark. In Arequipa, my face got lighter. It was nicer. It made me look like I was from the city.

Coata doesn't have electricity or water. Three years ago an expert from the city came to dig a well. My uncle worked for him. The well had a windmill that pumped the water up into a tank.

But the water was salty. It was only good for washing. So people didn't take care of the well and the windmill broke. Now there's no water. We have to haul it from the river.

Not too far from Coata there is an Inca fortress. One day my class went there on a field trip. I had never seen anything like it. There are towers built of huge stones. Tremendous stones! Inside the towers they found bones. The towers were tombs.

I had read about these things in school, but I never believed them. People say the Incas lifted those tremendous stones. Not even five of us could lift one. The Incas could do anything. They were strong. They worked hard. They were united.

Then the Spaniards came to Peru. They killed the Inca leaders and made the people work for them.

People aren't united now. In Coata, the mayor doesn't get along with the district governor. The judge doesn't get along with the mayor because he

wanted to be the mayor. Nobody cares about the
town. They only care about themselves.

I'm tired of living here. I want to go to the city.
I want to study. I'd like to become an engineer.
Then I could do something for Coata. Build schools
and parks, and pave the streets. The town needs
electricity, water, a stadium.

Then, once in a while, I would come back to Coata to visit.

I don't know what heaven is like. But I think heaven must be like a city. Because everybody is happy there. Nobody goes hungry. There are plenty of fruits. There is no water problem.

I don't know if it's true. But it could be.

I RETURNED TO COATA a year after my first visit to do more photographing and to make sure I had gotten Modesto's words right. I stayed with the Quispe family another four days and nights in the same adobe hut. This time I took more ponchos and blankets and a better sleeping bag.

Modesto and his brother had grown up a lot. Modesto was finishing sixth grade at a school in a town seven kilometers down the road. He talked excitedly about the possibility of going to Lima, the capital, to live with a family as their houseboy and attend secondary school there at night.

Romoldo was taking more after his father. One night in my hut, Juan played traditional Indian tunes on the flute and Romoldo accompanied him, playing "drums" on a tin can. Modesto left the room.

Santusa was as shy as ever and had not learned much more Spanish in school. Melania and Celestina were as playful as before and still loved my empty, bright-yellow Kodak film boxes.

This time I got to know Modesto's grandfather, Honorato. He didn't speak a word of Spanish, but we communicated by smiling. A smile goes a long way. When he smiled, he showed his crooked teeth, stained green from chewing coca leaves all his life.

The last day I was in Coata, the whole town got together at the handicraft center for the graduation of the first nursery school class. It was the result of the UNICEF project that had originally brought me to Coata. Melania was in the graduating class. Juan was in the band to play for the festivities.

People waited nearly two hours for the honored guests from the department of education to arrive from the city. Finally, the ceremony could wait no longer. The music began and the children danced. They danced well. The diplomas were handed out. Then refreshments were served.

The school principal and another man brought out a huge basket filled with the same triangular rolls we ate at breakfast. They passed out rolls, two to a person. When they got

to me, they passed by. I wondered: Do they think I'm too busy photographing, or do they think I don't need the food?

Then Celestina, not yet four, came up to me, holding out

the front of her skirt. In the fold was a single triangular roll.
She smiled. I took it, and smiled back.